A PRISONER IN THE CAUCASUS

BY

LYOF N. TOLSTOÏ

TRANSLATED FROM THE RUSSIAN

BY

NATHAN HASKELL DOLE

LYOF N. TOLSTOÏ

A PRISONER IN THE CAUCASUS

I.

A Russian of rank was serving as an officer in the army of the Caucasus. His name was Zhilin.

There came to him one day a letter from his home. His aged mother wrote him: "I am now getting along in years, and before I die I should like to see my beloved son. Come and bid me farewell, lay me in the ground, and then with my blessing return again to your service. And I have been finding a bride for you, and she is intelligent and handsome and has property. If you like, you can marry and settle down together."

Zhilin cogitated, "It is very true: the old lady has been growing feeble; maybe I shall not have a chance to see her again. Let us go, and if the bride is pretty—then I might marry."

He went to his colonel, got his leave of absence, took his farewell of his comrades, gave the soldiers of his command nine gallons of vodka as a farewell treat, and made his arrangements to depart.

There was war at that time in the Caucasus. The roads

were not open for travel either by day or night. If any of the Russians rode or walked outside of the fortress, the Tatars were likely either to kill him or carry him off to the mountains. And it was arranged that twice a week an escort of soldiers should go from fortress to fortress. In front and behind marched the soldiers, and the travellers rode in the middle.

It was now summer-time. At sunrise the baggage-train was made up behind the fortification; the guard of soldiery marched ahead, and the procession moved along the road.

Zhilin was on horseback, and his effects were on a cart that formed part of the train.

They had twenty-five versts to travel. The train marched slowly; sometimes the soldiers halted; sometimes a wagon-wheel came off, or a horse balked, and all had to stop and wait.

The sun was already past the zenith, but the train had only gone half way, so great were the dust and heat. The sun was baking hot, and nowhere was there shelter. A bald steppe; not a tree or a shrub on the road.

Zhilin rode on ahead, occasionally stopping and waiting till the train caught up with him. He would listen, and hear the signal on the horn to halt again. And Zhilin thought, "Would I better go on alone without the soldiers? I have a good horse under me; if I fall in with the Tatars, I can escape. Or shall I wait?"

He kept stopping and pondering. And just then another officer, also on horseback, rode up to him; his name was Kostuilin, and he had a musket.

He said, "Zhilin, let us ride on ahead together. I am so hungry that I cannot stand it any longer, and the heat too, —you could wring my shirt out!" Kostuilin was a heavy, stout, ruddy man, and the sweat was dripping from him.

Zhilin reflected, and said, "And your musket is loaded?"

"It is."

"All right, let us go. Only one condition: not to separate."

And they started on up the road. They rode along the steppe, talking and looking on each side. There was a wide sweep of view. As soon as the steppe came to an end, the road went into a pass between two mountains.

And Zhilin said, "I must ride up on that mountain, and reconnoitre, otherwise you see they might come down from the mountain and surprise us."

But Kostuilin said, "What is there to reconnoitre? Let us go ahead."

Zhilin did not heed him.

"No," says he, "you wait for me here below. I'll just glance around."

And he spurred his horse up the mountain to the left.

The horse that Zhilin rode was a hunter; he had bought him out of a drove of colts, paying a hundred rubles for him, and he had himself trained him. He bore him up the steep slope as on wings. He had hardly reached the summit when before him less than seven hundred feet distant mounted Tatars were standing,—thirty men.

He saw them, and started to turn back, but the Tatars had caught sight of him; they set out in pursuit of him, unstrapping their weapons as they gallop. Zhilin dashes down the precipice with all the speed of his horse, and cries to Kostuilin, "Fire your gun!" and to his horse he says, though not aloud, "Little mother, carry me safely, don't stumble; if you trip, I am lost. If we get back to the gun, we won't fall into their hands."

But Kostuilin, instead of waiting for him, as soon as he saw the Tatars, galloped on with all his might toward the fortress. With his whip he belabored his horse, first on one side, then on the other; all that could be seen through the dust, was the horse switching her tail.

Zhilin saw that his case was desperate. The gun was gone; nothing was to be done with a sabre alone. He turned his horse back toward the train; he thought he might escape that way.

But in front of him, he sees that six are galloping down the steep. His horse is good, but theirs are better; and besides, they have got the start of him. He started to wheel about, and was going to dash ahead again, but his horse had got momentum, and could not be held back; he flew straight down toward them.

He sees a red-bearded Tatar approaching him on a gray mare. He is gaining on him; he gnashes his teeth; he is getting his gun ready.

"Well," thinks Zhilin, "I know you devils; if you should take me prisoner, you would put me in a hole, and flog me with a whip. I won't give myself up alive."

Now, Zhilin was not of great size, but he was an uhlan. He drew his sabre, spurred his horse straight at the red-bearded Tatar. He says to himself, "Either I will crush him with my horse, or I will hack him down with my sabre."

Zhilin, however, did not reach the place on horseback; suddenly behind him, gun-shots were fired at the horse. The horse fell headlong, and pinned Zhilin's leg to the ground.

He tried to arise; but already ill-smelling Tatars were sitting on him, and pinioning his hands behind his back.

He burst from them, knocking the Tatars over; but three others had dismounted from their horses, and began to beat him on the head with their gun-stocks.

His sight failed him, and he staggered.

The Tatars seized him, took from their saddles extra saddle-girths, bent his arms behind his back, fastened them with a Tatar knot, and lifted him up.

They took his sabre from him, pulled off his boots, made a thorough search of him, pulled out his money and his watch, tore his clothes all to pieces.

Zhilin glanced at his horse. The poor beast lay as he had fallen, on his side, and was kicking, vainly trying to rise. In his head was a hole, and from the hole the black blood was pouring; the dust for an arshin around was wet with it.

A Tatar went to the horse to remove the saddle. He was still kicking, so the man took out his dagger, and cut his throat. The throat gave a whistling sound, a trembling ran over the body, and all was over.

The Tatars took off the saddle and the other trappings. The one with the red beard mounted his horse, and the others lifted Zhilin behind him to keep him from falling; they fastened him with the reins to the Tatar's belt, and thus they carried him off to the mountains.

Zhilin sat behind, swaying and bumping his face against the stinking Tatar's back.

All that he could see before him was the healthy Tatar back, and the sinewy neck, and a smooth-shaven nape, showing blue beneath the cap.

Zhilin's head ached; the blood trickled into his eyes. And it was impossible for him to get a more comfortable position on the horse, or wipe away the blood. His arms were so tightly bound that his collar-bones ached. They rode long from mountain to mountain; they forded a river; then they entered a highway, and rode along a valley. Zhilin tried to follow the route that they took him; but his eyes were glued together with blood, and it was impossible for him to turn round.

It began to grow dark; they crossed still another river, and began to climb a rocky mountain. There was an odor of smoke. The barking of dogs was heard.

They had reached an *aul*.

The Tatars dismounted. The Tatar children came running up, and surrounded Zhilin, whistling and exulting. Finally they began to fling stones at him.

The Tatar drove away the children, lifted Zhilin from the horse, and called a servant.

A Nogáï, with prominent cheek-bones, came at the call. He wore only a shirt. The shirt was torn; his whole breast was bare. The Tatar said something to him. The servant brought a foot-stock. It consisted of two oaken blocks provided with iron rings, and in one of the rings was a clamp with a lock. They unfastened Zhilin's arms, put on the stock, and took him to a barn, pushed him in, and shut the door.

Zhilin fell on the manure. As he lay there, he felt round in the darkness, and when he had found a place that was less foul, he stretched himself out.

II.

Zhilin scarcely slept that night. The nights were short. He saw through a crack that it was growing light. Zhilin got up, widened the crack, and managed to look out.

Through the crack he could see a road leading down from the mountain; at the right, a Tatar *saklia* with two trees near it. A black dog was lying on the road; a she-goat with her kids was walking by, all of them shaking their tails.

He saw coming down the mountain a young Tatar girl in a variegated shirt, ungirdled, in pantalettes and boots; her head was covered with a kaftan, and on it she bore a great tin water-jug.

She walked along, swaying and bending her back, and holding by the hand a little Tatar urchin, with shaven head, who wore a single shirt.

After the Tatar maiden had passed with her water-jug, the red-bearded Tatar of the evening before came out, wearing a silk beshmet, a silver dagger in his belt, and sandals on his bare feet. On his head was a high cap of sheep-skin, dyed black, and with the point hanging down. He came out, stretched himself, stroked his red beard. He paused, gave some order to the servant, and went off somewhere.

Then two children on horseback came along on their

way to the watering-trough. The hind-quarters of the horses were wet.

Other shaven-headed youngsters, with nothing but shirts on, and nothing on their legs, formed a little band, and came to the barn; they got a dry stick, and stuck it through the crack.

Zhilin growled "*ukh*" at them. The children began to cry, and scatter in every direction as fast as their legs would carry them; only their bare knees glistened. But Zhilin began to be thirsty; his throat was parched. He said to himself, "I wonder if they won't come to look after me?"

Suddenly the barn-doors are thrown open.

The red Tatar came in, and with him another, of slighter stature and of dark complexion. His eyes were bright and black, his cheeks ruddy, his little beard well trimmed, his face jolly and always enlivened with a grin.

The dark man's clothing was still richer: a silk beshmet of blue silk, embroidered with gold lace. In his belt, a great silver dagger; handsome morocco slippers embroidered with silver, and over the fine slippers he wore a larger pair of stout ones. His cap was tall, of white lamb's wool.

The red Tatar came in, muttered something, gave vent to some abusive language, and then stood leaning against the wall, fingering his dagger, and scowling under his brows at Zhilin, like a wolf.

But the dark Tatar, nervous and active, and always on the go, as though he were made of springs, came straight up to Zhilin, squatted down on his heels, showed his teeth, tapped him on the shoulder, began to gabble something in his own language, winked his eyes, and, clucking his tongue, kept saying, "A fine Russ, a fine Russ!"

Zhilin did not understand him, and said, "Drink; give me some water."

The dark one grinned.

"A fine Russ!" and all the time he kept babbling.

Zhilin signified by his hands and lips that they should give him water.

The dark one understood, grinned, put his head out of the door, and cried, "Dina!"

A young girl came running in,—a slender, lean creature of thirteen, with a face like the dark man's. Evidently she was his daughter.

She was dressed in a long blue shirt with wide sleeves and without a belt. On the bottom, on the breast, and on the cuffs it was relieved with red trimmings. She wore on her legs pantalettes and slippers, and over the slippers another pair with high heels. On her neck was a necklace wholly composed of half-ruble pieces. Her head was uncovered; she had her hair in a black braid, and on the braid was a ribbon, and to the ribbon were attached various ornaments and a silver ruble.

Her father gave her some command. She ran out, and quickly returned, bringing a little tin pitcher. After she had handed him the water, she also squatted on her heels in such a way that her knees were higher than her shoulders.

She sits that way, and opens her eyes, and stares at Zhilin while he drinks, as though he were some wild beast.

Zhilin offered to return the pitcher to her. She darted away like a wild goat. Even her father laughed.

He sent her after something else. She took the pitcher, ran out, and brought back some unleavened bread on a small round board, and again squatted down, and stared without taking her eyes from him.

The Tatars went out, and again bolted the door.

After a while the Nogáï also comes to Zhilin, and says, "*Aï-da, khozyáïn, aï-da!*"

But he does not know Russian either. Zhilin, however, perceived that he wished him to go somewhere.

Zhilin hobbled out with his clog; it was impossible to

walk, so he had to drag one leg. The Nogáï led the way for him.

He sees before him a Tatar village, of half a score of houses, and the native mosque with its minaret.

In front of one house stood three horses saddled. Lads held them by the bridle. From this house came the dark Tatar, and waved his hand, signifying that Zhilin was to come to him. He grinned, and kept saying something in his own tongue, and went into the house.

Zhilin followed him.

The room was decent; the walls were smoothly plastered with clay. Against the front wall were placed featherbeds; on the sides hung costly rugs; on the rugs were guns, pistols, and sabres, all silver-mounted.

On one side a little oven was set in, on a level with the floor.

The floor was of earth, clean as a threshing-floor, and the whole of the front portion was covered with felt; rugs were distributed over the felt, and on the rugs were down pillows.

On the rugs were sitting some Tatars in slippers only,— the dark Tatar, the red-bearded one, and three guests. Behind their backs, down cushions were placed; and before them on wooden plates were pancakes of millet-flour, and melted butter in a cup, and the Tatar beer, called *buza*, in a pitcher. They ate with their fingers, and all dipped into the butter.

The dark man leaped up, bade Zhilin sit on one side, not on a rug but on the bare floor; going back again to his rug, he handed his guests cakes and *buza*.

The servant showed Zhilin his place; he himself took off his shoes, placed them by the door in a row with the slippers of the other guests, and took his seat on the felt as near as possible to his masters; and while they eat he looks at them, and his mouth waters.

After the Tatars had finished eating, a Tatar woman entered, dressed in the same sort of shirt as the girl wore, and in pantalettes; her head was covered with a handkerchief. She carried out the butter and the cakes, and brought a handsome finger-bowl, and a pitcher with a narrow nose.

The Tatars finished washing their hands, then they folded their arms, knelt down, and puffed on all sides, and said their prayers. They talked in their own tongue.

Then one of the guests, a Tatar, approached Zhilin, and began to speak to him in Russian. "Kazi Muhamet made you prisoner," said he, pointing to the red-bearded Tatar; "and he has given you to Abdul Murat," indicating the dark one. "*Abdul Murat is now your master.*"

Zhilin said nothing.

Abdul Murat began to talk, all the time pointing toward Zhilin, and grinned as he talked-: "*soldat Urus, korosho*

Urus."

The interpreter went on to say, "He commands you to write a letter home, and have them send money to ransom you. As soon as money is sent, he will set you free."

Zhilin pondered a little, and then said, "Does he wish a large ransom?"

The Tatars took counsel together, and then the interpreter said,—

"Three thousand silver rubles."

"No," replied Zhilin, "I can't pay that."

Abdul leaped up, began to gesticulate and talk to Zhilin; he seemed all the time to think that Zhilin understood him.

The interpreter translated his words. "He means," says he, "how much will you give?"

Zhilin after pondering a little said, "Five hundred rubles."

Then the Tatars all began to talk at once. Abdul began to scream at the red-bearded Tatar. He grew so excited as he talked, that the spittle flew from his mouth.

But the red-bearded Tatar only frowned, and clucked with his tongue.

When all became silent again, the interpreter said, "Five hundred rubles is not enough to buy you of your master. He himself has paid two hundred for you. Kazi Muhamet was in debt to him. He took you for the debt. Three thousand rubles; it is no use to send less. But if you don't write, they will put you in a hole, and flog you with a whip."

"*Ekh!*" thinks Zhilin, "the more cowardly one is, the worse it is for him." He leaped to his feet, and said,—

"Now you tell him, dog that he is, that if he thinks he is going to frighten me, then I will not give him a single kopek nor will I write. I am not afraid of you, and you will never make me afraid of you, you dog!" The interpreter translated this, and again they all began to talk at once.

They gabbled a long time, then the dark one got up and came to Zhilin.

"*Urus,*" says he, "*jigit, jigit Urus!*"

The word *jigit* among them signifies a brave young man. And he grinned, said something to the interpreter, and the interpreter said, "Give a thousand rubles." Zhilin would not give in. "I will not pay more than five hundred. But if you kill me, you will get nothing at all."

The Tatars consulted together, sent out the servant, and they themselves looked first at the door, then at Zhilin.

The servant returned, followed by a rather stout man in

bare feet and almost stripped. His feet also were in stocks.

Zhilin made an exclamation: he recognized Kostuilin.

And they brought him in, and placed him next his comrade; the two began to talk together, and the Tatars looked on and listened in silence.

Zhilin told how it had gone with him; Kostuilin told how his horse had stood stock still, and his gun had missed fire, and that this same Abdul had overtaken him and captured him.

Abdul listened, pointed to Kostuilin, and muttered something. The interpreter translated his words to mean that they now both belonged to the same master, and that the one who paid the ransom first would be freed first. "Now," says he to Zhilin, "you lose your temper so easily, but your comrade is calm; he has written a letter home; they will send five thousand silver rubles. And so he will be well fed, and he won't be hurt."

And Zhilin said, "Let my comrade do as he pleases. Maybe he is rich. But I am not rich; I will do as I have already told you. Kill me if you wish, but it would not do you any good, and I will not pay you more than five hundred rubles."

They were silent.

Suddenly Abdul leaped up, brought a little chest, took out a pen, a sheet of paper, and ink, and pushed them into Zhilin's hands, then tapped him on the shoulder, and said by signs, "Write." He had agreed to take the five hundred rubles.

"Wait a moment," said Zhilin to the interpreter. "Tell him that he must feed us well, clothe us, and give us good decent foot-wear, and let us stay together. We want to have a good time. And lastly, that he take off these clogs."

He looked at his Tatar master, and smiled. The master also smiled, and when he learned what was wanted, said, —

"I will give you the very best clothes: a cherkeska and boots, fit for a wedding. And I will feed you like princes. And if you want to live together, why, you can live in the barn. But it won't do to take away the clogs: you would run away. Only at night will I have them taken off." Then he jumped up, tapped him on the shoulder: "You good, me good."

Zhilin wrote his letter, but he put on it the wrong address so that it might never reach its destination. He said to himself, "I shall run away."

They took Zhilin and Kostuilin to the barn, strewed corn-stalks, gave them water in a pitcher, and bread, two old cherkeski, and some worn-out military boots. It was evident that they had been stolen from some dead soldier. When night came they took off their clogs, and locked them up in the barn.

III.

Thus Zhilin and his comrade lived a whole month. Their master was always on the grin.

"You, Iván, good—me, Abdul, good."

But he gave them wretched food; unleavened bread made of millet-flour, cooked in the form of cakes, but often not heated through.

Kostuilin wrote home again, and was anxiously awaiting the arrival of the money, and lost his spirits. Whole days at a time, he sat in the barn, and counted the days till his money should arrive, or else he slept.

But Zhilin had no expectation that his letter would reach its destination, and he did not write another.

"Where," he asked himself,—"where would my mother get the money for my ransom? And besides, she lived for the most part on what I used to send her. If she made out to raise five hundred rubles, she would be in want till the end of her days. If God wills it, I may escape."

And all the time he kept his eyes open, and made plans to elude his captors.

He walked about the aul; he amused himself by whistling; or else he sat down and fashioned things, either modelling dolls out of clay or plaiting baskets of osiers, for Zhilin was a master at all sorts of handiwork.

One time he had made a doll with nose, and hands and feet, and dressed in a Tatar shirt, and he set the doll on the roof. The Tatar women were going for water. Dina, the master's daughter, caught sight of the doll. She called the Tatar girls. They set down their jugs, and looked and laughed.

Zhilin took the doll, and offered it to them. They keep laughing, but don't dare to take it.

He left the doll, went to the barn, and watched what would take place.

Dina ran up to the doll, looked around, seized the doll, and fled.

The next morning at dawn he sees Dina come out on the doorstep with the doll. And she has already dressed it up in red rags, and was rocking it like a little child, and singing a lullaby in her own language.

An old woman came out, gave her a scolding, snatched the doll away, broke it in pieces, and sent Dina to her work.

Zhilin made another doll, a still better one, and gave it to Dina.

One time Dina brought a little jug, put it down, took a seat, and looked at him. Then she laughed, and pointed to the jug.

"What is she so gay about?" thinks Zhilin.

He took the jug, and began to drink. He supposed that it was water, but it was milk.

He drank up the milk.

"Good," says he. How delighted Dina was! "Good, Iván, good!"

And she jumped up, clapped her hands, snatched the jug, and ran away. And from that time she began to bring him secretly fresh milk every day.

Now, sometimes the Tatars would make cheesecakes out of goat's milk, and dry them on their roofs. Then she used to carry some of these cakes secretly to him. And another time, when her father had killed a sheep, she brought him a piece of mutton in her sleeve. She threw it down, and ran away.

One time there was a tremendous shower, and for a whole hour the rain poured as from buckets; and all the brooks grew roily. Wherever there had been a ford, the depth of the water increased to seven feet, and bowlders were rolled along by it. Everywhere torrents were rushing, the mountains were full of the roaring.

Now, when the shower was over, streams were pouring all through the village. Zhilin asked his master for a knife, whittled out a cylinder and some paddles, and made a water-wheel, and fastened manikins at the two ends.

The little girls brought him some rags, and he dressed up

the manikins, one like a man, the other like a woman. He fastened them on, and put the wheel in a brook. The wheel revolved, and the dolls danced.

The whole village collected: the little boys and the little girls, the women, and even the Tatars, came and clucked with their tongues. "*Aï, Urus! aï, Iván!*"

Abdul had a Russian watch, which had been broken. He took it, and showed it to Zhilin, and clucked with his tongue. Zhilin said,—

"Let me have it, I will fix it."

He took it, opened the penknife, took it apart. Then he put it together again, and gave it back. The watch ran.

The Tatar was delighted, brought him his old beshmet which was all in rags, and gave it to him. Nothing else to be done,—he took it, and used it as a covering at night.

From that time, Zhilin's fame went abroad, that he was a "master." Even from distant villages, they came to him. One brought him a gun-lock or a pistol to repair, another a watch.

His master furnished him with tools,—a pair of pincers and gimlets and a little file.

One time a Tatar fell ill; they came to Zhilin: "Come cure him!"

Zhilin knew nothing of medicine. He went, looked at the

sick man, said to himself, "Perhaps he will get well, anyway." He went into the barn, took water and sand, and shook them up together. He whispered a few words to the water in presence of the Tatars, and gave it to the sick man to drink.

Fortunately for him, the Tatar got well.

Zhilin had by this time learned something of their language. And some of the Tatars became accustomed to him; when they wanted him, they called him by name, "Iván, Iván;" but others always looked at him as though he was a wild beast.

The red-bearded Tatar did not like Zhilin; when he saw him, he scowled and turned away, or else insulted him.

There was another old man among them; he did not live in the aul, but came down from the mountain. Zhilin never saw him except when he came to the mosque to prayer. He was of small stature; on his cap, he wore a white handkerchief as an ornament. His beard and mustaches were trimmed; they were white as wool, and his face was wrinkled and brick-red. His nose was hooked like a hawk's, and his eyes were gray and cruel, and he had no teeth except two tusks.

He used to come in his turban, leaning on his staff, and glare like a wolf; whenever he saw Zhilin, he would snort, and turn his back.

One time Zhilin went to the mountain to see where the old man lived. He descended a narrow path, and sees a little stone-walled garden. On the other side of the wall are cherry-trees, peach-trees, and a little hut with a flat roof.

He went nearer; he sees bee-hives made of straw, and bees flying and humming around them. And the old man is on his knees before the hives, hammering something.

Zhilin raised himself up, so as to get a better view, and his clog made a noise.

The old man looked up,—squealed; he pulled his pistol from his belt, and fired at Zhilin, who had barely time to hide behind the wall.

The old man came to make his complaint to Zhilin's master. Abdul called him in, grinned, and asked him:

"Why did you go to the old man's?"

"I didn't do him any harm. I wanted to see how he lived."

Abdul explained it to the old man; but he was angry, hissed, mumbled something, showed his tusks, and threatened Zhilin with his hands.

Zhilin did not understand it all; but he made out that the old man wished Abdul to kill the two Russians, and not have them in the aul.

The old man went off.

Zhilin began to ask his master, "Who is that old man?" And the master replied,—

"He is a great man. He used to be our first *jigit*; he has killed many Russians. He used to be rich. He had three wives and eight sons. All lived in one village. The Russians came, destroyed his village, and killed seven of his sons. One son was left, and surrendered to the Russians. The old man went and gave himself up to the Russians also. He lived among them three months, found his son, killed him with his own hand, and escaped. Since that time he has stopped fighting. He went to Mecca to pray to God, and that's why he wears a turban. Whoever has been to Mecca is called a *hadji*, and wears a *chalma*. But he does not love you Russians. He has bade me kill you, but I don't intend to kill you. I have paid out money for you, and besides, Iván, I have come to like you. And so far from wishing to kill you, I would rather not let you go from me at all, if I had not given my word."

He laughed, and began to repeat in Russian, "*Tvoyá Iván, khorósh, moyá, Abdul, khorósh.*"

IV.

Thus Zhilin lived a month. In the daytime he walked about the aul or did some handiwork, but when night came, and it grew quiet in the aul, he burrowed in his barn. It was hard work digging because of the stones, and he sometimes had to use his file on them; and thus he dug a hole under the wall big enough to crawl through.

"Only," he thought, "I must know the region a little first,

so as to escape in the right direction. And the Tatars wouldn't tell me any thing."

He waited till one time when his master was absent, then he went after dinner behind the aul to a mountain. His idea was to reconnoitre the country.

But when Abdul returned he commanded a small boy to follow Zhilin, and not take his eyes from him. The little fellow tagged after Zhilin, and kept crying,—

"Don't go there. Father won't allow it. I will call the men if you go!"

Zhilin began to reason with him. "I am not going far," says he,—"only to that hill: I must get some herbs. Come with me; I can't run away with this clog. To-morrow I will make you a bow and arrows."

He persuaded the lad, they went together. To look at, the mountain is not far, but it was hard work with the clog; he went a little distance at a time, pulling himself up by main strength.

Zhilin sat down on the summit, and began to survey the ground.

To the south behind the barn lay a valley through which a herd was grazing, and another aul was in sight at the foot of it. Back of the village was another hill still steeper, and back of that still another. Between the mountains lay a further stretch of forest, and then still other mountains constantly rising higher and higher. And higher than all, stood snow-capped peaks white as sugar, and one snowy peak rose like a dome above them all.

To the east and west also were mountains. In every direction the smoke of auls was to be seen in the ravines.

"Well," he said to himself, "this is all their country."

He began to look in the direction of the Russian possessions. At his very feet was a little river, his village surrounded by gardens. By the river some women, no larger in appearance than little dolls, were standing and washing. Behind the aul was a lower mountain, and beyond it two other mountains covered with forests. And between the two mountains a plain stretched far, far away in the blue distance; and on the plain lay what seemed like smoke.

Zhilin tried to remember in what direction, when he lived at home in the fortress, the sun used to rise, and where it set. He looked. "Just about there," says he, "in that valley, our fortress ought to be. There, between those two mountains, I must make my escape."

The little sun began to slope toward the west. The snowy mountains changed from white to purple; the wooded mountains grew dark; a mist arose from the valley; and the valley itself, where the Russian fortress must be, glowed in the sunset as though it were on fire. Zhilin strained his gaze. Something seemed to hang waving in the air, like smoke arising from chimneys.

And so it seemed to him that it must be from the fortress

itself,—the Russian fortress.

It was already growing late. The voice of the mulla calling to prayer was heard. The herds began to return; the kine were lowing. The little lad kept repeating, "Let us go!" but Zhilin could not tear himself away.

They returned home.

"Well," thinks Zhilin, "now I know the place; I must make my escape."

He proposed to make his escape that very night. The nights were dark; it was the wane of the moon.

Unfortunately the Tatars returned in the evening. Usually they came in driving the cattle with them, and came in hilarious. But this time they had no cattle; but they brought a Tatar, dead on his saddle. It was Kazi Muhamet's brother. They rode in solemnly, and collected for the burial.

Zhilin also went out to look.

They did not put the dead body in a coffin, but wrapped it in linen, and placed it under a plane-tree in the village, where it lay on the sward.

The mulla came; the old men gathered together, their caps bound around with handkerchiefs. They took off their shoes, and sat in rows on their heels before the dead.

In front was the mulla, behind him three old men in turbans, and behind them the rest of the Tatars. The mulla lifted the dead man's head, and said, "Allah!" (That means God.) He said this one word, and let the head fall back. All were silent; they sat motionless.

Again the mulla lifted the head, saying, "Allah!" and all repeated it after him,—

"Allah!"

Then silence again.

The dead man lay on the sward; he was motionless, and they sat as though they were dead. Not one made a motion. The only sound was the rustling of the foliage of the plane-tree, stirred by the breeze.

Then the mulla offered a prayer. All got to their feet; they took the dead body in their arms, and carried it away.

They brought it to a pit. The pit was not a mere hole, but was hollowed out under the earth like a cellar.

They took the body under the armpits and by the legs, doubled it up, and let it down gently, shoved it forcibly under the ground, and laid the arms along the belly. The Nogáï brought a green osier. They laid it in the pit; then they quickly filled it up with earth, and over the dead man's head they placed a gravestone. They smoothed the earth over, and again sat around the grave in rows. There was a long silence.

A PRISONER IN THE CAUCASUS

"Allah! Allah! Allah!"

They sighed and got up. The red-bearded Tatar gave money to the old men, then he got up, struck his forehead three times with a whip, and went home.

The next morning Zhilin sees the red-haired Tatar leading a mare through the village, and three Tatars following him. They went behind the village. Kazi Muhamet took off his beshmet, rolled up his sleeves,—his hands were powerful,—took out his dagger, and sharpened it on a whetstone. The Tatars held back the mare's head. Kazi Muhamet approached, and cut the throat; then he turned the animal over, and began to flay it, pulling away the hide with his mighty fists.

The women and maidens came, and began to wash the intestines and the lights. Then they cut up the mare, and carried the meat to the hut. And the whole village collected at the Kazi Muhamet's to celebrate the dead.

For three days they feasted on the mare and drank *buza*. Thus they celebrated the dead. All the Tatars were at home.

On the fourth day about noon, Zhilin sees that they are collecting for some expedition. Their horses are brought out. They put on their gear, and started off, ten men of them, under the command of the Kazi Muhamet; only Abdul staid at home. There was a new moon, but the nights were still dark.

"Now," thinks Zhilin, "to-day we must escape." And he

tells Kostuilin.

But Kostuilin was afraid. "How can we escape? We don't know the way."

"I know the way."

"But we should not get there during the night."

"Well, if we don't get there we will spend the night in the woods. I have some cakes. What are you going to do? It will be all right if they send you the money, but you see, your friends may not collect so much. And the Tatars are now angry because the Russians have killed one of their men. They say they are thinking of killing us."

Kostuilin thought and thought. "All right, let us go!"

V.

Zhilin crept down into his hole, and widened it so that Kostuilin also could get through, and then they sat and waited till all should be quiet in the aul.

As soon as the people were quiet in the aul, Zhilin crept under the wall, and came out on the other side. He whispers to Kostuilin, "Crawl under."

Kostuilin also crept under, but in doing so he hit a stone with his leg, and it made a noise.

Now, the master had a brindled dog as a watch,—a most ferocious animal; they called him Ulyashin.

Zhilin had been in the habit of feeding him. Ulyashin heard the noise, and began to bark and jump about, and the other dogs joined in.

Zhilin gave a little whistle, threw him a piece of cake. Ulyashin recognized him, began to wag his tail, and ceased barking.

Abdul had heard the disturbance, and cried from within the hut:—

"*Háït! háït!* Ulyashin."

But Zhilin scratched the dog behind the ears. The dog makes no more sound, rubs against his legs, and wags his tail.

They wait behind the corner.

All became silent again; the only sound was the bleating of a sheep in the fold, and far below them the water roaring over the pebbles.

It is dark, but the sky is studded with stars. Over the mountain the young moon hung red, with its horns turned upward.

In the valleys a mist was rising, white as milk. Zhilin started up, and said to his comrade in Tatar, "Well, brother, *aï-da!*"

They set out again.

But as they get under way, they hear the call of the mulla

on the minaret:—

"*Allah! Bis'm Allah! el Rakhman!*"

"That means, the people will be going to the mosque."

Again they sat down and hid under the wall.

They sat there long, waiting until the people should pass. Again it grew still.

"Now for our fate!"

They crossed themselves, and started.

They went across the dvor, and down the steep bank to the stream, crossed the stream, proceeded along the valley. The mist was thick, and closed in all around them, but above their heads the stars could still be seen.

Zhilin used the stars to guide him which way to go. It was cool in the mist, it was easy walking, only their boots were troublesome,—they were worn at the heels. Zhilin took his off, threw them away, and walked barefoot. He sprang from stone to stone, and kept glancing at the stars.

Kostuilin began to grow weary. "Go slower," says he; "my boots chafe me, my whole foot is raw."

"Then take them off, it will be easier."

Kostuilin began to go barefoot, but that was still worse; he kept scraping his feet on the stones and having to stop.

Zhilin said to him, "You may cut your feet, but you will save your life; but if you are caught they will kill you, which would be worse."

Kostuilin said nothing, but crept along, groaning. For a long time they went down the valley. Suddenly they hear dogs barking at the right. Zhilin halted, looked around, climbed up the bank, and felt about with his hands.

"*Ekh!*" says he, "we have made a mistake; we have gone too far to the right. Here is one of the enemy's villages. I could see it from the hill. We must go back to the left, up the mountain. There must be a forest there."

But Kostuilin objected. "Just wait a little while, let us get breath. My feet are all blood."

"Eh, brother! they will get well. You should walk more lightly. This way."

And Zhilin turned back toward the left, and up hill toward the forest.

Kostuilin kept halting and groaning. Zhilin tried to hush him up, and still hastened on.

They climbed the mountain. And there they found the forest. They entered it; their clothes were all torn to pieces on the thorns. They found a little path through the woods. They walked along it.

"Halt!"

There was the sound of hoofs on the path. They stopped to listen. It sounded like the tramping of a horse: then it also stopped. They set out once more; again the tramping hoofs. When they stopped, it stopped.

Zhilin crept ahead, and investigated a light spot on the path.

Something is standing there. It may be a horse, or it may not, but on it there is something strange, not at all like a man.

It snorted—plainly! "What a strange thing!"

Zhilin gave a slight whistle. There was a dash of feet from the path into the forest, a crackling in the underbrush, and something rushed along like a hurricane, with a crashing of dry boughs.

Kostuilin almost fell to the ground in fright. But Zhilin laughed, and said,—

"That was a stag. Do you hear how it crashes through the woods with its horns? We frightened him, and he frightened us."

They went on their way. Already the Great Bear was beginning to set; the dawn was not distant. And they were in doubt whether they should come out right or not. Zhilin was inclined to think that they were on the right track, and that it would be about ten versts farther before they reached the Russian fortress, but there is no certain guide; you could not tell in the night.

They came to a little clearing. Kostuilin sat down and said,—

"Do as you please, but I will not go any farther; my legs won't carry me."

Zhilin tried to persuade him.

"No," says he, "I won't go, I can't go."

Zhilin grew angry; he threatens him, he scolds him.

"Then I will go on without you. Good-by!"

Kostuilin jumped up and followed. They went four versts farther. The fog began to grow thicker in the forest. Nothing could be seen before them; the stars were barely visible.

Suddenly they hear the tramping of a horse just in front of them; they can hear his shoes striking on the stones.

Zhilin threw himself down on his belly, and tried to listen by laying his ear to the ground.

"Yes, it is,—it is some one on horseback coming in our direction."

They slipped off to one side of the road, crouched down in the bushes, and waited. Zhilin crept close to the path, and looked.

He sees a mounted Tatar riding along, driving a cow. The man is muttering to himself. When the Tatar had ridden by, Zhilin returned to Kostuilin.

"Well, God has saved us. Up with you! Come along!"

Kostuilin tried to rise, and fell back.

"I can't; by God, I can't. My strength is all gone."

The man was as though he were drunk. He was all of a sweat; and as they were surrounded by the cold fog, and his feet were torn, he was quite used up. Zhilin tried to lift him by main force. Then Kostuilin cried, "*Aï!* it hurt."

Zhilin was frightened to death.

"What are you screaming for? Don't you know that Tatar is near? He will hear you." But he said to himself, "Now he is really played out, what can I do with him? I can't abandon a comrade. Now," says he, "get up; climb on my back. I will carry you if you can't walk any longer." He took Kostuilin on his shoulders, holding him by the thighs, and went along the path with his burden. "Only," says he, "don't put your hands on my throat, for Christ's sake! Lean on my shoulders."

It was hard for Zhilin. His feet were also bloody, and he was weary. He stopped, and made it a little easier for himself by setting Kostuilin down, and getting him better mounted. Then he went on again.

Evidently the Tatar had heard them when Kostuilin screamed. Zhilin caught the sound of some one following them and shouting in his language. Zhilin put into the bushes. The Tatar aimed his gun; he fired it off, but missed; began to whine in his native tongue, and galloped up the path.

"Well," says Zhilin, "we are lost, brother. The dog,—he will be right back with a band of Tatars on our track.... If we don't succeed in putting three versts between us, we are lost." And he thinks to himself, "The devil take it, that I had to bring this clod along with me! Alone, I should have got there long ago."

Kostuilin said, "Go alone. Why should you be lost on my account?"

"No, I will not go; it would not do to abandon a comrade." He lifted him again on his shoulder, and started on. Thus he made a verst. It was forest all the way, and no sign of outlet. But the fog was now beginning to lift, and seemed to be floating away in little clouds: not a star could be seen. Zhilin was tired out.

A little spring gushed out by the road: it was walled in with stones. There he stopped, and dropped Kostuilin.

"Let me rest a little," says he, "and get a drink. We will eat our cakes. It can't be very far now."

He had just stretched himself out to drink, when the sound of hoofs was heard behind them. Again they hid in the bushes at the right under the crest, and crouched down.

They heard Tatar voices. The Tatars stopped at the very spot where they had turned in from the road. After discussing a while, they seemed to be setting dogs on the scent.

The refugees hear the sound of a crashing through the bushes: a strange dog comes directly to them. He stops and barks.

The Tatars followed on their track. They are also strangers.

They seized them, bound them, lifted them on horses, and carried them off.

After they had ridden three versts, Abdul, with two Tatars, met them. He said something to their new captors. They were transferred to Abdul's horses, and were brought back to the aul.

Abdul was no longer grinning, and he said not a word to them.

They reached the village at daybreak; the prisoners were left in the street. The children gathered around them, tormenting them with stones and whips, and howling.

The Tatars gathered around them in a circle, and the old man from the mountain was among them. They began to discuss. Zhilin made out that they were deciding on what should be done with them. Some said that they ought to be sent farther into the mountains, but the old man declared that they must be killed. Abdul argued against it. Says he, "I have paid out money for them, I shall get a ransom for them."

But the old man said, "They won't pay any thing; it will only be an injury to us. And it is a sin to keep Russians alive. Kill them, and that is the end of it."

They separated. Abdul came to Zhilin, and reported the decision.

"If," says he, "the ransom is not sent in two weeks, you will be flogged. And if you try to run away again, I will kill you like a dog. Write your letter, and write it good!"

Paper was brought them; they wrote their letters. Clogs were put on their feet again; they were taken behind the mosque.... There was a pit twelve feet deep, and they were thrust down into this pit.

VI.

Life was made utterly wretched for them. Their clogs were not taken off even at night, and they were not let out at all.

Unbaked dough was thrown down to them as though they were dogs, and water was let down in a jug. In the pit it was damp and suffocating.

Kostuilin became ill, and swelled up, and had rheumatism all over his body, and he groaned or slept all the time.

Even Zhilin lost his spirits; he sees that they are in desperate straits. And he does not know how to get out.

He had begun to make an excavation, but there was nowhere to hide the earth; Abdul discovered it, and threatened to kill him.

He was squatting down one time in the pit, and thinking about life and liberty, and he grew sad.

Suddenly a cake fell directly into his lap, then another, and some cherries followed. He looked up, and there was Dina. She peered down at him, laughed, and then ran away. And Zhilin began to conjecture, "Couldn't Dina help me?"

He cleared out a little place in the pit, picked up some clay, and made some dolls. He made men and women, horses and dogs; he said to himself, "When Dina comes, I will give them to her."

But Dina did not make her appearance on the next day. And Zhilin hears the trampling of horses' hoofs: men came riding up: the Tatars collected at the mosque, arguing, shouting, and talking about the Russians.

The voice of the old man was heard. Zhilin could not

understand very well, but he made out that the Russians were somewhere near, and the Tatars were afraid that they would attack the aul, and they did not know what to do with the prisoners.

They talked a while, and went away. Suddenly Zhilin heard a rustling at the edge of the pit.

He sees Dina squatting on her heels, with her knees higher than her head; she leaned over, her necklace hung down and swung over the pit. And her little eyes twinkled like stars. She took from her sleeve two cheesecakes, and threw them down to him. Zhilin accepted them, and said, "Why did you stay away so long? I have been making you some dolls. Here they are." He began to toss them up to her one at a time.

But she shook her head, and would not look at them. "I can't take them," said she. She said nothing more for a time, but sat there: then she said, "Iván, they want to kill you."

She made a significant motion across her throat.

"Who wants to kill me?"

"Father. The old man has ordered him to. But I am sorry for you."

And Zhilin said, "Well, then, if you are sorry for me, bring me a long stick." She shook her head, meaning that it was impossible.

He clasped his hands in supplication to her. "Dina, please! Bring one to me, Dínushka!"

"I can't," said she. "They would see me; they are all at home." And she ran away.

Afterwards, Zhilin was sitting there in the evening, and wondering what he should do. He kept raising his eyes. He could see the stars, but the moon was not yet up. The mulla uttered his call, then all became silent.

Zhilin began already to doze, thinking to himself, "The little maid is afraid."

Suddenly a piece of clay fell on his head; he glanced up; a long pole was sliding over the edge of the pit, it slid out, began to descend toward him, it reached the bottom of the pit. Zhilin was delighted. He seized it, pulled it along,—it was a strong pole. He had noticed it before on Abdul's roof.

He gazed up; the stars were shining high in the heavens, and Dina's eyes, at the edge of the pit, gleamed in the darkness like a cat's.

She craned her head over, and whispered, "Iván, Iván." And she waved her hands before her face, meaning, "Softly, please."

"What is it?" said Zhilin.

"All have gone, there are only two at home."

And Zhilin said, "Well, Kostuilin, let us go, let us make our last attempt. I will help you."

Kostuilin, however, would not hear to it.

"No," says he, "it is not meant for me to get away from here. How could I go when I haven't even strength to turn over?"

"All right, then. Good-by. Don't think me unkind."

He kissed Kostuilin.

He clasped the pole, told Dina to hold it firmly, and tried to climb up. Twice he fell back,—his clog so impeded him. Kostuilin boosted him; he managed to get to the top: Dina pulled on the sleeves of his shirt with all her might, laughing heartily.

Zhilin pulled up the pole, and said, "Carry it back to its place, Dina, for if they found it they would flog you."

She dragged off the pole, and Zhilin began to go down the mountain. When he had reached the bottom of the cliff, he took a sharp stone, and tried to break the padlock of his clog. But the lock was strong; he could not strike it fairly.

He hears some one hurrying down the hill, with light, skipping steps. He thinks, "That is probably Dina again."

Dina ran to him, took a stone, and says, "Let me try it."

She knelt down, and began to work with all her might.

But her hands were as delicate as osiers. She had no strength. She threw down the stone, and burst into tears.

Zhilin again tried to break the lock, and Dina squatted by his side, and leaned against his shoulder. Zhilin glanced up, and saw at the left behind the mountain a red glow like a fire; it was the moon just rising.

"Well," he says to himself, "I must cross the valley and get into the woods before the moon rises." He stood up, and threw away the stone. No matter for the clog—he must take it with him.

"Good-by," says he. "Dínushka, I shall always remember you."

Dina clung to him, reached with her hands for a place to stow away some cakes. He took the cakes.

"Thank you," said he: "you are a thoughtful darling. Who will make you dolls after I am gone?" and he stroked her hair.

Dina burst into tears, hid her face in her hands, and scrambled up the hillside like a kid. He could hear, in the darkness, the jingling of the coins on her braids.

Zhilin crossed himself, picked up the lock of his clog so that it might not make a noise, and started on his way, dragging his leg all the time, and keeping his eyes constantly on the glow where the moon was rising.

He knew the way. He had eight versts to go in a direct

course, but he would have to strike into the forest before the moon came entirely up. He crossed the stream, and now the light was increasing behind the mountain.

He proceeded along the valley: it was growing light. He walks along, constantly glancing around; but still the moon was not visible. The glow was now changing to white light, and one side of the valley grew brighter and brighter. The shadow crept away from the mountain till it reached its very foot.

Zhilin still hurried along, all the time keeping to the shadow.

He hurries as fast as he can, but the moon rises still faster; and now, at the right, the mountain-tops are illuminated.

He struck into the forest just as the moon rose above the mountains. It became as light and white as day. On the trees all the leaves were visible. It was warm and bright on the mountain-side; every thing seemed as though it were dead. The only sound was the roaring of a torrent far below. He walked along in the forest; he had met no one. Zhilin found a little spot in the forest where it was still darker, and began to rest.

While he rested he ate one of his cakes. He procured a stone and once more tried to break the padlock, but he only bruised his hands, and failed to break the lock.

He arose and went on his way. When he had gone a verst his strength gave out, his feet were sore. He had to walk ten steps at a time, and then rest.

"There's nothing to be done for it," says he to himself. "I will push on as long as my strength holds out; for if I sit down, then I shall not get up again. If I do not reach the fortress before it is daylight, then I will lie down in the woods and spend the day, and start on to-morrow night again."

He walked all night. Once he passed two Tatars on horseback, but he heard them at some distance, and hid behind a tree.

Already the moon was beginning to pale, the dew had fallen, it was near dawn, and Zhilin had not reached the end of the forest.

"Well," says he to himself, "I will go thirty steps farther, strike into the forest, and sit down."

He went thirty steps, and sees the end of the forest. He went to the edge; it was broad daylight. Before him, as on the palm of his hand, were the steppe and the fortress; and on the left, not far away on the mountain-side, fires were burning, or dying out; the smoke rose, and men were moving around the watch-fires.

He looks, and sees the gleaming of fire-arms: Cossacks, soldiers!

Zhilin was overjoyed.

He gathered his remaining strength, and walked down

the mountain. And he says to himself, "God help me, if a mounted Tatar should get sight of me on this bare field! I should not escape him, even though I am so near." Even while these thoughts are passing through his mind, he sees at the left, on a hillock not fourteen hundred feet away, three Tatars on the watch. They caught sight of him,—bore down upon him. Then his heart failed within him. Waving his arms, he shouted at the top of his voice, "Brothers! help, brothers!"

Our men heard him,—mounted Cossacks dashed out toward him. The Cossacks were far off, the Tatars near. And now Zhilin collected his last remaining energies, seized his clog with his hand, ran toward the Cossacks, and, without any consciousness of feeling, crossed himself and cried, "Brothers, brothers, brothers!"

The Cossacks were fifteen in number.

The Tatars were dismayed. Before they reached him, they stopped short. And Zhilin reached the Cossacks.

The Cossacks surrounded him, and questioned him: "Who are you?" "What is your name?" "Where did you come from?"

But Zhilin was almost beside himself; he wept, and kept on shouting, "Brothers, brothers!"

The soldiers hastened up, and gathered around him; one brought him bread, another kasha-gruel, another vodka, another threw a cloak around him, still another broke his chains.

The officers recognized him, they brought him into the fortress. The soldiers were delighted, his comrades pressed into Zhilin's room.

Zhilin told them what had happened to him, and he ended his tale with the words,—

"That's the way I went home and got married! No, I see that such is not to be my fate."

And he remained in the service in the Caucasus.

At the end of a month Kostuilin was ransomed for five thousand rubles.

He was brought home scarcely alive.

Printed in Great Britain
by Amazon